CALIFORNIA
NATIVE AMERICAN TRIBES

TUBATULABAL
TRIBE

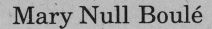

by

Mary Null Boulé

Book Twenty-one in a series of twenty-six

Dear Reader,

You will find an outline of this chapter's important topics at the back of the booklet. It is there for you to use in writing a report or giving an oral report on this tribe.

If you first read the booklet completely, then you can use the outline as a guide to write your report in your own words, instead of copying sentences from the chapter.

Good luck, read carefully, and use your own words.

MNB

Cover Illustration: Daniel Liddell

CALIFORNIA NATIVE AMERICAN TRIBES

TUBATULABAL TRIBE

by
Mary Null Boulé

Illustrated by
Daniel Liddell

Merryant Publishing
Vashon, Washington

Book Number Twenty-one in a series of twenty-six

This series is dedicated to Virginia Harding, whose editing expertise and friendship brought this project to fruition.

ISBN: 1-877599-24-7

Copyright © 1992, Merryant Publishing

7615 S.W. 257th St., Vashon, WA 98070.

FOREWORD

Native American people of the United States are often living their lives away from major cities and away from what we call the mainstream of life. It is, then, interesting to learn of the important part these remote tribal members play in our everyday lives.

More than 60% of our foods come from the ancient Native American's diet. Farming methods of today also can be traced back to how tribal women grew crops of corn and grain. Many of our present day ideas of democracy have been taken from tribal governments. Even some 1,500 Native American words are found in our English language today.

Fur traders bought furs from tribal hunters for small amounts of money, sold them to Europeans and Asians for a great deal of money, and became rich. Using their money to buy land and to build office buildings, some traders started business corporations which are now the base of our country's economy.

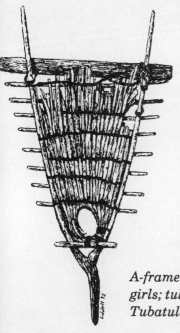

There has never been enough credit given to these early Americans who took such good care of our country when it was still in their care. The time has come to realize tribal contributions to our society today and to give Native Americans not only the credit, but the respect due them.

Mary Boulé

A-frame cradle for girls; tule matting. Tubatulabal tribe.

GENERAL INFORMATION

Out of Asia, many thousands of years ago, came Wanderers
Some historians think they were the first people to set foot
on our western hemisphere. These Wanderers had walked
step by step, onto our part of the earth while hunting and
gathering food. They probably never even knew they had
moved from one continent to another as they made their
way across a land bridge, a narrow strip of land between
Siberia and what is now Russia, and the state of Alaska.

Historians do not know exactly how long ago the Wanderers
might have crossed the land bridge. Some of them say
35,000 years ago. What historians do know is that these
people slowly moved down onto land that we now call the
United States of America. Today it would be very hard to
follow their footsteps, for the land bridge has been covered
with sea water since the thawing of the ice age.

Those Wanderers who made their way to California were
very lucky, indeed. California was a land with good weather
most of the year and was filled with plenty of plant and
animal foods for them to eat.

The Wanderers who became California's Native Americans
did not organize into large tribes like the rest of the North
American tribes. Instead, they divided into groups, or tribelets,
sometimes having as many as 250 people. A tribelet could
number as few as three, to as many as thirty villages
located close to each other. Some tribelets had only one
chief, a leader who lived in the largest village. Many tribes
had a chief for each village. Some leaders had no real power
but were thought to be wise. Tribal members always
listened with respect to what their chief had to say.

From 20 to 100 people could be living in one village, which
usually had several houses. In most cases, these groups of
people were related to each other. From five to ten people of
one family lived in one house. For instance, a mother, a

father, two or three children, a grandmother, or aunt or daughter-in-law might live together.

Village members together would own the land important to them for their well-being. Their land might include oak trees with precious acorns, streams and rivers, and plants which were good to eat. Streams and rivers were especially important to a tribe's quality of life. Water drew animals to it; that meant more food for the tribe to eat. Fish were a good source of food, and traveling by boat was often easier than walking long distances. Water was needed in every part of tribal life.

Village and tribelet land was carefully guarded. Each group knew exactly where the boundaries of its land were found. Boundaries were known by landmarks such as mountains or rivers, or they might also be marked by poles planted in the ground. Some boundary lines were marked by rocks, or by objects placed there by tribal members. The size of a territory had to be large enough to supply food to every person living there.

The California tribes spoke many languages. Sometimes villages close together even had a problem understanding one another. This meant that each group had to be sure of the boundaries of other tribes around them when gathering food. It would not be wise to go against the boundaries and the customs of neighbors. The Native Americans found if they respected the boundaries of their neighbors, not so many wars had to be fought. California tribes, in spite of all their differences, were not as warlike as other tribes in our country.

Not only did the California tribes speak different languages, but their members also differed in size. Some tribes were very tall, almost six feet tall. The shortest people came from the Yuki tribe which had territory in what is now Mendocino County. They measured only about 5'2" tall. All Native Americans, regardless of size, had strong, straight black hair and dark brown eyes.

TRADE

Trading between tribes was an important part of life. Inland tribes had large animal hides that coastal tribes wanted. By trading the hides to coastal groups, inland tribes would receive fish and shells, which they in turn wanted. Coastal tribes also wanted minerals and rocks mined in the mountains by inland tribes. Obsidian rock from the northern mountains was especially wanted for arrowheads. There were, as well, several minerals, mined in the inland mountains, which could be made into the colorful body paints needed for religious ceremonies.

Southern tribes particularly wanted steatite from the Gabrielino tribe. Steatite, or soapstone, was a special metal which allowed heat to spread evenly through it. This made it a good choice to be used for cooking pots and flat frying pans. It could be carved into bowls because of its softness and could be decorated by carving designs into it. Steatite came from Catalina Island in the Coastal Gabrielino territory. Gabrielinos found steatite to be a fine trading item to offer for the acorns, deerskins, or obsidian stone they needed.

When people had no items to trade but needed something, they used small strings of shells for money. The small dentalium shells, which came from the far distant Northwest coast, had great value. Strings of dentalia usually served as money in the Northern California tribes, although some dentalia was used in the Central California tribes.

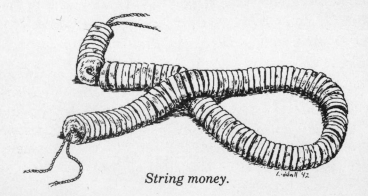

String money.

In southern California clam shells were broken and holes were bored through the center of each piece. Then the pieces were rounded and polished with sandstone and strung into strings for money. These were not thought to be as valuable as dentalia.

Strings of shell money were measured by tattoo marks on the trader's lower arm or hand.

Here is a sample of shell value:

A house, three strings
A fishing place, one to three strings
Land with acorn-bearing oak trees, one to five strings

A great deal of rock and stone was traded among the tribes for making tools. Arrows had to have sharp-edged stone for tips. The best stone for arrow tips was obsidian (volcanic glass) because, when hit properly, it broke off into flakes with very sharp edges. California tribes considered obsidian to be the most valuable rock for trading.

Some tribes had craftsmen who made knives with wooden handles and obsidian blades. Often the handles were decorated with carvings. Such knives were good for trading purposes. Stone mortars and pestles, used by the women for grinding grains into flour, were good trading items.

BASKETS & POTTERY

California tribal women made beautiful baskets. The Pomo and Chumash baskets, what few are left, show us that the women of those tribes might have been some of the finest basketmakers in the world. Baskets were used for gathering and storing food, for carrying babies, and even for hauling water. In emergencies, such as flooding waters, sometimes children, women, and tribal belongings crossed the swollen rivers and streams in huge, woven baskets! Baskets were so tightly woven that not a drop of water could leak from them.

Baskets also made fine cooking pots. Very hot rocks were taken from a fire and tossed around inside baskets with a looped tree branch until food in the basket was cooked.

Most baskets were made to do a certain job, but some baskets were designed for their beauty alone and were excellent for trading. Older women of a tribe would teach young girls how to weave baskets.

Pottery was not used by many California tribes. What little there was seems to have been made by those tribes living near to the Navaho and Mohave tribes of Arizona, and it shows their style. For example, pottery of the California tribes did not have much decoration and was usually a dull red color. Designs were few and always in yellow.

Ohlone hunter wearing deerskin camouflage.

Long thin coils of clay were laid one on top the other. Then the coils were smoothed between a wooden paddle and a small stone to shape the bowl. Pottery from California Native Americans has been described as light weight and brittle (easily broken), probably because of the kind of clay soil found in California.

HUNTING & FISHING

Tribal men spent much of their time making hunting and fishing tools. Bows and arrows were built with great care, to make them shoot as accurately as possible. Carelessly made hunting weapons caused fewer animals to be killed and people then had less food to eat.

Bows made by men of Southern California tribes were made long and narrow. In the northern part of the state bows were a little shorter, thinner, and wider than those of their northern neighbors. Size and thickness of bows depended on the size trees growing in a tribe's territory. The strongest bows were wrapped with sinew, the name given to animal tendons. Sinew is strong and elastic like a rubber band.

Arrows were made in many sizes and shapes, depending on their use. For hunting larger animals, a two-piece arrow was used. The front piece of the arrow shaft was made so that it would remain in the animal, even if the back part was removed or broken off. The arrowhead, or point, was wrapped to the front piece of the shaft. This kind of arrow was also used in wars.

Young boys used a simple wooden arrow with the end sharpened to a point. With this they could hunt small animals like birds and rabbits. The older men of the tribe taught boys how to make their own arrows, how to aim properly, and how to repair broken weapons.

Tribal men spent many hours making and mending fishing nets. The string used in making nets often came from the fibers of plants. These fibers were twisted to make them strong and tough, then knotted into netting. Fences, or weirs, that had one small opening for fish, were built across streams. As the fish swam through the opening they would be caught in netting or harpooned by a waiting fisherman.

Hooks, if used at all, were cut from shells. Mostly hooks could be found when the men fished in large lakes or when catching trout in high mountain areas. Hooks were attached to heavy plant fiber string.

Dip nets, made of netting attached to branches that were bent into a circle, were used to catch fish swimming near shore. Dip nets had long handles so the fishermen could reach deep into the water.

Sometimes a mild poison was placed on the surface of shallow water. This confused the fish and caused them to float to the surface of the water, where they could be scooped up by a waiting fisherman. Not enough poison was used to make humans ill.

Not all fishing was done from the shore. California tribes used two kinds of boats when fishing. Canoes, dug out of one half a log, were useful for river fishing. These were square at each end, round on the bottom, and very heavy. Some of them were well-finished, often even having a carved seat in them.

Today we think of "balsa" as a very lightweight wood, but in Spanish, the word balsa means "raft". That is why Spanish explorers called the Native American canoes, made from tule reeds, "balsa" boats.

Balsa boats were made of bundled tule reeds and were used throughout most of California. They made into safe, light-weight boats for lake and river use. Usually the balsa canoe had a long, tightly tied bundle of tule for the boat bottom and one bundle for each side of the canoe. The front of the canoe was higher than the back. Balsa boats could be steered with a pole or with a paddle, like a raft.

Men did most of the fishing, women were in charge of gathering grasses, seeds, and acorns for food. After the food was collected, it was either eaten right away or made ready for winter storage.

Except for a few southern groups, California tribes had perma-nent villages where they lived most of the year. They also had food-gathering places they returned to each year to collect acorns, salt, fish, and other foods not found near their villages.

FOOD

Many different kinds of plant food grew wild in California in the days before white people arrived. Berries and other plant foods grew in the mountains. Forests offered the local tribes everything from pine nuts to animals.

Native Americans found streams full of fish for much of the year. Inland fresh water lakes had large tule reeds growing along their shores. Tule could be eaten as food when plants were young and tender. More important, however, tule was used in making fabric for clothes and for building boats and houses. Tule was probably the most useful plant the California Native Americans found growing wild in their land.

Like all deserts, the one in southern California had little water or fish, but small animals and cactus plants made good food for the local tribes. They moved from place to place harvesting whatever was ripe. Tribal members always knew when and where to find the best food in their territory.

Acorns were the main source of food for all California tribes. Acorn flour was as important to the California Native Americans as wheat is to us today. Five types of California oak trees produced acorns that could be eaten. Those from black oak and tanbark oak seem to have been the favorite kinds.

Since some acorns tasted better than others, the tastiest ones were collected first. If harvest of the favorite acorn was poor some years, then less tasty acorns had to be eaten all winter long.

So important were acorns to California Indians that most tribes built their entire year around them. Acorn harvest marked the beginning of their calendar year. Winter was counted as so many months after acorn harvest, and summer was counted by the number of months before the next acorn harvest.

Acorn harvest ceremonies usually were the biggest events of the year. Most celebrations took place in mid-October and included dancing, feasts, games of chance, and reunions with relatives. Harvest festivals lasted for many days. They were a time of joy for everyone.

The annual acorn gathering lasted two to three weeks. Young boys climbed the oak trees to shake branches; some men used long poles to knock acorns to the ground. Women loaded the nuts into large cone-shaped burden baskets and carried them to a central place where they were put in the sun to dry.

Once the acorns were dried, the women carried them back to the tribe's permanent villages. There they lined special basket-like storage granaries with strong herbs to keep insects away, then stored the acorns inside. Granaries were placed on stilts to keep animals from getting into them and were kept beside tribal houses.

Preparing acorns for each meal was also the women's job. Shells were peeled by hitting the acorns with a stone hammer on an anvil (flat) stone. Meat from the nut was then laid on a stone mortar. A mortar was usually a large stone with a slight dip on its surface. Sometimes the mortar had a bottomless basket, called a hopper, glued to its top. This kept the acorn meat from sliding off the mortar as it was beaten. The meat was then pounded with a long stone pestle. Acorn flour was scraped away from the hopper's sides with a soaproot fiber brush during this process.

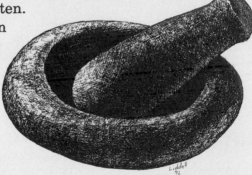

From there the flour was put into an open-worked basket and sifted. A fine flour came through the bottom of the basket, while the larger pieces were put back in the mortar for more pounding.

The most important process came after the acorn flour was sifted. Acorn flour has a very bitter-tasting tannin in it. This bitter taste was removed by a method called leaching. Many tribes leached the flour by first scooping out a hollow in sand near water. The hollow was lined with leaves to keep the flour from washing away. A great deal of hot water was poured through the flour to wash out (leach) the bitterness. Sometimes the flour was put into a basket for the leaching process, instead of using sand and leaves.

Finally the acorn flour was ready to be cooked. To make mush, heated stones were placed in the basket with the flour. A looped tree branch or two long sticks were used to toss the hot rocks around so the basket would not burn. When the mush had boiled, it could be eaten. If the flour and water mixture was baked in an earthen oven, it became a kind of bread. Early explorers wrote that it was very tasty.

Historians have estimated that one family would eat from 1500 to 2000 pounds of acorn flour a year. One reason California native Americans did not have to plant seeds and raise crops was because there were so many acorns for them to harvest each year.

Whether they ate fish or shellfish or plant food or animal meat, nature supplied more than enough food for the Native Americans who lived in California long ago. Many believed their good fortune in having fine weather and plenty to eat came from being good to their gods.

RELIGION

Tribal members had strong beliefs in the power of spirits or gods around them. Each tribe was different, but all felt the importance of never making a spirit angry with them. For that reason a celebration to thank the spirit-gods for treating them well, took place before each food gathering and before each hunting trip, and after each food harvest.

Usually spiritual powers were thought to belong to birds or animals. Most California tribespeople felt bears were very wicked and should not be eaten. But Coyote seems to have been a kind leader who helped them if they were in trouble, even though he seems to have been a bit naughty at times. Eagle was thought to be very powerful and good to native Americans. In some tribes, Eagle was almost as powerful as Sun.

Tribes placed importance on different gods, according to the tribe's needs. Rain gods were the most important spirits to desert tribes. Weather gods, who might bring less rain or warmer temperatures, were important to northern tribes. A great many groups felt there were gods for each of the winds: North, South, East and West. The four directions were usually included in their ceremonial dances and were used as part of the decorations on baskets, pots, and even tools.

Animals were not only worshipped and believed to be spirit-gods, like Deer or Antelope, but tribal members felt there was a personal animal guardian for each one of them. If a tribal member had a deer as guardian, then that person could never kill a deer or eat deer meat.

California Native Americans believed in life after death. This made them very respectful of death and very fearful of angering a dead person. Once someone died, the name of the dead person could never again be said aloud. Since it was easy to accidentally say a name aloud, the name was usually given to a new baby. Then the dead person would not become angry.

Shamans were thought to be the keepers of religious beliefs and to have the ability to talk directly to spirit-gods. It was the job of a village shaman to cure sick people, and to speak to the gods about the needs of the people. Some tribes had several kinds of shamans in one village. One shaman did curing, one scared off evil spirits, while another took care of hunters.

Not all shamans were nice, so people greatly feared their power. However, if shamans had no luck curing sick people or did not bring good luck in hunting, the people could kill them. Most shamans were men, but in a few tribes, women were doctors.

Most California tribal myths have been lost to history because they were spoken and never written down. The legends were told and retold on winter nights around the home fires. Sadly, these were forgotten after the missionaries brought Christianity to California and moved tribal members into the missions.

A few stories still remain, however. It is thought by historians that northwest California tribes were the only ones not to have a myth on how they were created. They did not feel that the world was made and prepared for human beings. Instead, their few remaining stories usually tell of mountain peaks or rivers in their own territory.

The central California tribes had creation stories of a great flood where there was only water on earth. They tell of how man was made from a bit of mud that a turtle brought up from the bottom of the water.

Many southwest tribes believed there was a time of no sky or water. They told of two clouds appearing which finally became Sky and Earth.

Throughout California, however, all tribes had myths that told of Eagle as the leader, Coyote as chief assistant, and of less powerful spirits like Falcon or Hawk.

Costumes for religious ceremonies often imitated these animals they worshipped or feared. Much time was spent in making the dance costumes as beautiful as possible. Red woodpecker feathers were so brilliant a color they were used to decorate religious headdresses, necklaces, or belts. Deerskin clothing was fringed so shell beads could be attached to each thin strip of leather.

Eagle feathers were felt to be the most sacred of religious objects. Sometimes they were made into whole robes.

Religious feather charm.

Usually, though, the feathers were used just for decorations. All these costumes were valuable to the people of each tribe. The village chief was in charge of taking care of the costumes, and there was terrible punishment for stealing them. Clothing worn everyday was not fancy like costuming for rituals.

Willow bark skirt.

CLOTHING

Central and southern California's fine weather made regular clothes not really very important to the Native Americans. The children and men went naked most of the year, but most women wore a short apron-like skirt. These skirts were usually made in two pieces, front and back aprons, with fringes cut into the bottom edges. Often the skirt was made from the inner bark of trees, shredded and gathered on a cord. Sometimes the skirt was made from tule or grass.

In northern California and in rainy or windy weather elsewhere in the state, animal-skin blankets were worn by both men and women. They were used like a cape and wrapped around the body. Sometimes the cape was put over

17

one shoulder and under the other arm, then tied in front. All kinds of skins were used; deer, otter, wildcat, but sea-otter fur was thought to be the best. If the skin was from a small animal, it was cut into strips and woven together into a fabric. At night the cape became a blanket to keep the person warm.

Because of the rainy weather in northern California, the women wore basket caps all the time. Women of the central and south tribes wore caps only when carrying heavy loads, where the forehead had to be used as support. Then a cap helped keep too much weight from being placed on the forehead.

Most California people went barefoot in their villages. For journeys into rough land, going to war, wood gathering, or in colder weather, the tribesmen in central and northwest California wore a one-piece soft shoe with no extra sole, which went high up on the leg.

Southern California tribespeople, however, wore sandals most of the time, wearing high, soled moccasins only when they traveled long distances or into the mountains. Leggings of skin were worn in snow, and moccasins were sometimes lined with grass for more comfort and warmth.

VILLAGE LIFE

Houses of the California tribes were made of materials found in their area. Usually they were round with domed roofs. Except for a few tribes, a house floor was dug into the earth a few feet. This was wise, for it made the home warmer in winter and cooler in summer. It also meant that less material was needed to make house walls.

Framework for the walls was made from bendable branches tied to support poles. Some frames of the houses were covered with earth and grass. Others were covered with large slabs of redwood or pine bark. Central California

Split-stick clapper, rhythm instrument. Hupa tribe.

villagers made large woven mats of tule reed to cover the tops and sides of houses. In the warmer southern area, brush and smaller pieces of bark were used for house walls.

Most California Native American villages had a building called a sweathouse, where the men could be found when they were not hunting, fishing or traveling. It was a very important place for the men, who used it rather like a clubhouse. They could sweat and then scrape themselves clean with curved ribs of deer. The sweathouse was smaller than a family house. Normally it had a center pole framework with a firepit on the ground next to the pole. When the fire was lit, some smoke was allowed to escape through a hole at the top of the roof; however, most was trapped inside the building. Smoke and heat were the main reasons for having a sweathouse. Both were believed to be a way to purify tribal members' bodies. Sweathouse walls were mainly hard-packed earth. The heat produced was not a steam heat but came from a wood-fed fire.

In the center of most villages was a large house that often had no walls, just a roof held up with poles. It was here that religious dances and rituals were held, or visitors were entertained.

Dances were enjoyed and were performed with great skill. Music, usually only rhythm instruments, accompanied the dances. For some reason California Native Americans did not use drums to create rhythms for their dances. Three different kinds of rattles were used by California tribes.

One type, split-clap sticks, created rhythm for dancing. These were usually a length of cane (a hollow stick) split in half lengthwise for about two-thirds of its length. The part still uncut was tightly wound with cord so it would not split all the way. The stick was held at the tied end in one hand and hit against the palm of the other hand to make its sound.

19

A pebble-filled moth cocoon made rhythm for shaman duties. These could range from calling on spirits to cure illnesses, to performing dances to bring rain. Probably the best sounds to beat rhythm for songs and dances came from bundles of deer hooves tied together on a stick. These rattles have a hollow, warm sound.

The only really "musical" instrument found in California was a flute made of reed that was played by blowing across the edge of one end. Melodies were not played on any of these instruments. Most North American Indians sang their songs rather than playing melodies on music instruments.

Special songs were sung for each event. There were songs for healing sick people, songs for success in hunting, war, or marriage. Women sang acorn-grinding songs and lullabies. Songs were sung in sorrow for the dead and during story-telling times. Group singing, with a leader, was the favorite kind of singing. Most songs were sung by all tribe members, but religious songs had to be sung by a special group. It was important that sacred songs not be changed through the years. If a mistake was made while singing sacred music, the singer could be punished, so only specially trained singers would sing ritual songs.

All songs were very short, some of them only 20 to 30 seconds long. They were made longer by repeating the melodies over and over, or by connecting several songs together. Songs usually told no story, just repeated words or phrases or syllables in patterns.

Song melodies used only one or two notes and harmony was never added. Perhaps that is why mission Indians, at those missions with musician priests, especially loved to sing harmony in the church choirs.

Songs and dances were good methods of passing rich tribal traditions on to the children. It was important to tribal adults that their children understand and love the tribe's heritage.

Children were truly wanted by parents in most tribes and new parents carefully watched their tiny babies day and night, to be sure they stayed warm and dry. Usually a newborn was strapped into a cradle and tied to the mother's back so she could continue to work, yet be near the baby at all times. In some tribes, older children took care of babies of cradle age during the day to give the mother time to do all her work, while grandmothers were often in charge of caring for toddlers.

Children were taught good behavior, traditions, and tribal rules from babyhood, although some tribes were stricter than others. Most of the time parents made their children obey. Young children could be lightly punished, but in many tribes those over six or seven years old were more severely punished if they did not follow the rules.

Just as children do today, Native American youngsters had childhood traditions they followed. For instance, one tribal tradition said that when a baby tooth came out, a child waited until dusk, faced the setting sun and threw the tooth to the west. There is no mention of a generous tooth fairy, however.

Tribal parents were worried that their offspring might not be strong and brave. Some tribes felt one way to make their children stronger was by forcing them to bathe in ice cold water, even in wintertime. Every once in a while, for example, Modoc children were awakened from sleep and taken to a cold lake or stream for a freezing bath.

But if freezing baths at night were hard on young Native Americans, their days were carefree and happy. Children were allowed to play all day, and some tribes felt children did not even have to come to dinner if they didn't want to. In those tribes, children could come to their houses to eat anytime of the day.

The games boys played are not too different from those played today. Swimming, hide and seek among the tule reeds, a form of tetherball with a mud ball tied to a pole, and willow-javelin throwing kept boys busy throughout the day.

Fathers made their sons small bows and arrows, so boys spent much time trying to improve their hunting skills. They practised shooting at frogs or chipmunks. The first animal any boy killed was not touched or eaten by him. Others would carry the kill home to be cooked and eaten by villagers. This tradition taught boys always to share food.

Another hunting tool for boys was a hollowed-out willow branch. This became like a modern day beanshooter, only the Native American boys shot juniper berries instead of beans. Slingshots made good hunting weapons, as well.

Girls and boys shared many games, but girls playing with each other had contests to see who could make a basket the fastest, or they played with dolls made of tule. Together, young boys and girls played a type of ring-around-the-rosie game, climbed mountains, or built mud houses.

As children grew older, the boys followed their fathers and the girls followed their mothers as the adults did their daily work. Children were not trained in the arts of hunting or basketmaking, however, until they became teenagers.

HISTORY

Spanish missionaries, led by Fray Junipero Serra, arrived in California in 1769 to build missions along the coast of California. By 1823, fifty years later, 21 missions had been founded. Almost all of them were very successful, and the Franciscan monks who ran them were proud of how many Native Americans became Christians.

However, all was not as the monks had planned it would be. Native American people had never been around the diseases European white men brought with them. As a result, they had no immunity to such illnesses as measles, small pox, or flu. Too many mission Indians died from white men's diseases.

Historians figure there were 300,000 Native Americans living in California before the missionaries came. The missions show records of 83,000 mission Indians during mission days. By the time the Mexicans took over the missions from the Spanish in 1834, only 20,000 remained alive.

The great California Gold Rush of 1849 was probably another big reason why many of the Native Americans died during that time. White men, staking their claim to tribal lands with gold upon it, thought nothing of killing any California tribesman who tried to keep and protect his territory. Fifty-thousand tribal members died from diseases, bullets, or starvation between the gold Rush Days and 1870. By 1910, only 17,000 California Indians remained.

Although the American government tried to set aside reservations (areas reserved for Native Americans), the land given to the Indians often was not good land. Worse yet, some of the land sacred to tribes, such as burial grounds, was taken over by white people and never given back.

Sadly, mission Indians, when they became Christians, forgot the proud heritage and beliefs they had followed for thousands of years. Many wonderful myths and songs they had passed from one generation to the next, on winter nights so long ago, have been lost forever.

Today some 100,000 people can claim California Native American ancestors, but few pure-blooded tribespeople remain. Our link with the Wanderers, who came from Asia so long ago, has been forever broken.

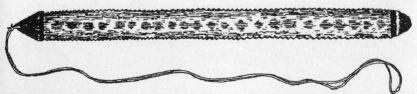

The bullroarer made a deep, loud sound when whirled above the player's head. Tipai tribe.

Villages were usually built beside a lake, stream, or river. Balsa canoes are on the shore. Tule reeds grow along the edge of the water and are drying on poles on the right side of the picture.

Women preparing food in baskets, sit on tule mats. Tule mats are being tied to the willow pole framework of a house being built by one of the men.

TUBATULABAL TRIBE

INTRODUCTION

The name Tubatulabal (Two bottle' ball—say this five times, please, while looking at the word) means 'pine nut eaters' and was given to this tribe by the neighboring Yokut tribe. Tubatulabal people lived along the banks of the Kern and South Fork Kern Rivers, in the south Sierra Nevada foothills region. Ancient tribal territory went from Mount Shasta in the north to 40 miles south of where the river and its south fork came together.

The land today is almost unchanged from tribal times. The northern two-thirds of old Tubatulabal territory is mountainous, with elevations from 2,500 feet to 14,500 feet above sea level. Between mountains in this area are many high-valley grass meadows and small lakes, along with sparse evergreen forests.

The southern one-third of old tribal territory has three connecting valleys, the Kern valley, South Fork Kern valley, and Hot Springs valley. These valleys are hot and dry in the summer with temperatures often reaching from 100° to 115°.

Winters in these southern valleys are mostly cold and rainy, with temperatures ranging from freezing (32°) to a much warmer 70°. Snow sometimes falls in the higher parts of the valleys during winter. The taller mountains in this area, however, are covered with snow from November to March.

Plants growing in the three southern valleys are almost like true desert plants. There are cacti, dry grasslands, and manzanita bushes. Scrub oak, willow, and cottonwood trees survive in this hot, dry region. Juniper and pine trees grow in the upper edges of the South Fork Kern Valley Oak and sugar pine trees are found in Kern Valley.

All territory boundary lines, during ancient times, were kept well-marked. Natural boundary marks, like big rock outcroppings or mountain peaks, were used by the tribelets in marking their territory. However, each tribelet allowed the others of their tribe to search for food in its area without the need for permission.

Little is known about these people before 1850. Tribal members claim to have always lived in the Kern valley. Myths told by Tubatulabal storytellers do not speak of moving into the valley.

There were three tribelets, or groups, of Tubatulabal people. They spoke a language all three groups could understand. Even though there was a feeling of loyalty in times of war, with the groups joining together against an enemy, the tribelets lived completely separate lives.

VILLAGES

Instead of having one permanent village, these tribespeople had several homes throughout the year, settling in one place for several months only in the winter. Winter villages were small, having two to six families living in them. Dwellings were round, domed, single-family buildings. House walls needed to be only brush covered with mud.

Winter dwellings were furnished with floor mats woven of tule cane, beds with tule mattresses, and blankets of deer-and bearskins. Storage baskets and other belongings were also found inside a home.

At nut-gathering campsites, in the fall of the year, several families lived together in a large, round, roofless area surrounded by brush. The brush walls were from three to four feet high, and the whole enclosure was from 30 to 50 feet in diameter.

By making the living area so large, it could be used for ceremonies and dance events, as well as a home. A special area of this campsite was cleared so guests and performers coming to ceremonies could camp there during the celebrations.

During warmer weather, the villagers built shelters with brush roofs to shade them from the hot sun. The roofs were held up by four poles with two horizontal roof beams keeping the poles steady. This shelter had no walls. Families worked, ate, and slept under their shelters.

A brush hut made by saplings pulled together and covered with buckskin for shade.

Sweathouse.

Most villages had sweathouses. These buildings were large and oval-shaped with a framework of oak branches. The side walls and roof were made of logs and poles, which were first covered with brush, then with dirt.

Sweating was done in the evenings, with men and women going to the sweathouse separately. The building was heated by a large wood fire. Steam was not used to heat bodies.

A sweathouse was usually placed near a pool of water or a dammed stream; when those sweating became too hot, they could jump into the nearby cool water. Villagers believed sweating would purify their bodies.

VILLAGE LIFE

Tubatulabal families were made up of parents, unmarried children, widowed parents, sons-in-law, and sometimes daughters-in-law. All villagers were usually related to each other in some way.

The jobs of hunting and fishing were left mostly to the men of a village. Women were in charge of jobs which took more time but were probably less physical.

According to a tribal myth, the reason for dividing work this way was the result of an ancient contest. A Tubatulabal myth tells of how, at the beginning of time, the choices of jobs were decided. An arrow-shooting contest between men and women was arranged by Coyote, with the winner to be forever in charge of hunting and fishing.

Because of tricks played by Coyote to help the men, women lost this important arrow-shooting contest. Therefore, men were always to do the hunting and fishing; women were to gather and prepare plant foods, make baskets and clothing, and mind the children. In spite of the myth, both men and women worked together for piñon-nut gathering and the annual group-fishing event.

There were several kinds of marriages within this tribe. Sometimes a marriage was arranged by two sets of parents while their children were still babies. Usually this kind of marriage was to unite two wealthy families so as to combine their wealth. The children did not marry until they were grown.

Another kind of marriage was that of a young couple choosing each other as partners. In this type of marriage, the groom's parents paid a bride price of clamshell money to the bride's parents. In return, the bride's parents gave gifts of baskets and acorns to the groom's family. Newlyweds, when the bride price had been paid, then lived in the groom's village.

A third kind of marriage was one in which a young man received permission from a young woman's parents to marry their daughter. The groom lived with the bride's family, helping them with hunting and fishing, until the couple's first baby was born. Then they moved to their own house.

Before a baby was born, the mother-to-be followed all tribal rules to make sure her baby was going to be healthy. She did not eat meat or use salt the last month before a baby was born. If a mother-to-be ate meat just before her baby's birth, villagers believed her husband would be unable to find deer when he went hunting for food for the mother and their new baby.

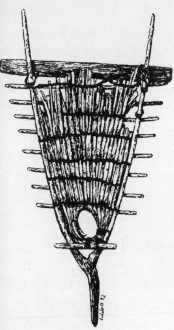

Y-shaped cradle with tule matting.

A baby was born in a specially dug hollow in the floor of the new parents' home. The infant stayed there for six days after birth. Warmed stones, covered by tule mats, lined the hollow, making it a warm, lovely place for a new baby to begin life.

The baby was put into a sitting cradle woven around a Y-shaped branch. The bottom of the Y had a point on it so that the cradle could be stuck into the ground near the mother, keeping the baby nearby as she worked.

Following tribal rules, the new mother and father ate no meat, grease, or salt for one month after the birth of their child. It was believed that by obeying this rule their baby would find favor with spirit powers around them.

Children nearly 200 years ago played together much as they do today. But time was also set aside for children to learn manners, tribal history from storytellers, and to learn, by watching, how adults did their jobs.

Young boys learned to use a bow and arrow by aiming wooden arrows with sharpened points at small animals, such as rabbits and squirrels. Girls learned basketmaking and food preparation by helping their mothers and grandmothers.

When a villager died, the body was kept overnight in the house where death took place. The next morning, two specially trained village women wrapped the dead body in tule mats and buried it in an oak grove some distance from the village.

One after-death ritual tribal members followed was called a 'face washing' ceremony, held sometime within the first year of a loved one's death. At this event, the closest living relative to a dead person had his or her face washed by a non-relative from another village.

Later, a mourning ceremony was held for all villagers who had died in the past year or two. A life-size image of each dead person was made for the ceremony. The event was often called Image Ceremony for this reason, but was really celebrated to mark the end of a long mourning period for relatives.

During the ritual six-day ceremony, the images, along with all belongings of the dead, were burned in a huge fire. Invited friends and relatives then feasted on food and enjoyed entertainment of dancing and singing for the rest of the time.

Tubatulabal (Remember? Two-bottle-ball) people believed that a soul left a body upon death and took the form of a human once again. This ghost human was believed to travel in dust devils during the daylight hours. Although most of the ghost spirits were thought to be harmless, some were felt to be quite evil.

Villages had no leader but each of the three tribelets had a chief who was in charge of the villages in his group. Chiefs were not all-powerful in the Tubatulabal tribe. Though a chief was not a very strong leader, tribal laws were extremely powerful in themselves, and were obeyed by villagers without question. Perhaps that is why leaders did not have to be so demanding.

Mostly chiefs gave advice to villagers, met with other tribelets and tribes in time of war, decided on the need for war, arranged peace agreements, and acted as good role models for their people.

Chiefs were appointed by elderly men from all the different villages in a tribelet. To be chosen, they needed to be over

40 years old, wealthy, to have good judgement, and to be honest, intelligent, and well-liked.

Usually, a dying chief named one of his sons, or a brother, to take his place. If the elderly men felt the dying chief's choice was a good one, they approved his decision.

If his choice turned out not to be a good enough leader, the second most powerful man in the tribelet, known as 'clown/dance-manager,' led the villagers in choosing another chief.

A Tubatulabal clown was like no other man of power in California tribes. He made people laugh during ceremonies by dancing backward and speaking nonsense words; but he could also make unkind remarks about a bad chief and use his 'clown' power to convince people they should choose a new leader.

Warrior with pole vest to protect his chest from enemy arrows.

WARS AND FEUDS

The most important job a chief had was being war chief. Wars with unfriendly neighboring tribes usually started over an act of revenge by one group against another. Revenge was felt necessary when a chief had been insulted by another chief or a fellow Tubatulabal tribal member had been killed by another village or tribelet. Wars lasted only a few days and there were usually not many deaths.

The tribe's style of war was to attack an enemy village in the early morning. A battle was fought all day, and when the warriors ran out of arrows, or when night fell, a battle ended and the attackers went home.

Sometimes, prisoners and dead enemies' weapons were taken back to the winning warriors' village to be shown to everyone.

RELIGION

The Tubatulabal people believed in many supernatural spirits. Spirits were thought to be in both human and animal form. Certain animals like Coyote, Bear, Deer, Rattlesnake, Owl, and Hawk were felt to be supernatural spirit-gods. Villagers felt sure that shamans, who were the spirit doctors of the village, had the ghosts of dead relatives as their helpers.

Shamans were the spiritual leaders of each village and both men and women could hold these jobs. Shamans had to be born with certain spiritual powers; practice alone could not make someone a shaman.

According to tribal laws, men shamans could have both supernatural power and the ability to cure sick people. Women were not allowed to be curing doctors, but could have supernatural power. All shamans had special spirit-guardian helpers. Curing shamans particularly used large birds and deer as spirit helpers. Coyotes, dead relatives' ghosts, and rattlesnakes were believed to be supernatural helpers for all shamans.

Curing shamans were looked up to in the village; the more people they cured the more important they became. These shamans felt their power came to them, when they needed it, through fasting (going without food for a period of time). They used curing songs, ritual dances, and herbal medicines to heal villagers.

Shamans also were called upon to reach spirits with requests for good weather, fine plant crops each year, and for enough rain to grow many plants.

Coyote was the mythical spirit that villagers prayed to in fearful worship. The reason they both feared and worshipped Coyote was that no one ever knew whether Coyote was going to be a hero or a rascal.

It was Tubatulabal belief that people's souls left their bodies when they had a dream. Every tribal member tried hard not to dream. Another belief was that myths could only be told by storytellers in the winter. If a myth was told at any other time, it was thought a rattlesnake could bite both listeners and tellers. Tubatulabal people were certain all bad luck and death (except for war deaths) came from evil spirits or witchcraft.

FOOD

The diet of this tribe was mainly plant foods and fish. Many different kinds of plants and grasses grew in their territory, and tribal members gathered as much as they could during each growing season.

Because piñon nuts could only be harvested every other year, six kinds of acorn nuts were gathered to fill in as the major tribal food. Acorns were collected from the ground beneath oak trees, then sun-dried, and stored in granaries built above the ground in winter villages.

Piñon cones were knocked down from pine trees, gathered into a large pile with brush, and set on fire to force the cones to break apart. After the cones spread open, the nuts could be removed and were sun-dried for storage. Piñon nuts were stored where they were gathered, in round stone-lined pits five feet across and two-and-one-half feet deep. Nut meats were ground into flour to make mush and bread.

Other foods Tubatulabal people gathered were small grass seeds, new shoots of plants, plant leaves, bulbs, and tubers (like potatoes). Seeds and wild berries were gathered by using seed-beater baskets, round, shallow baskets with handles. The seeds were ground into flour meal, using mortar and pestle, in much the same way as nut meats were ground.

Berries were boiled and ground into a mealy flour. Then the berry flour was mixed with water and shaped into cakes of dough, sun dried, and stored for winter. Whenever water was added to a piece of berry cake, it became a tasty drink all villagers enjoyed.

Salt came from the edges of dried salt-water lakes in the Mohave Desert.

Plants were eaten both fresh and cooked. Cooking meant either boiling, parching, roasting, or baking. Baking was done in pit ovens, which were holes in the ground lined with very hot rocks. Fish, such as trout, whitefish, catfish, and freshwater mussels were roasted in shells or over an open fire.

Boiling baskets were used to boil food. A mixture of water and food was placed in a boiling basket with hot stones, which were tossed about with sticks to keep the rocks from burning the basket.

Large animals like deer, antelope, bear, mountain lion, and

mountain sheep were skinned right after they were killed, while they were still warm. The meat was then brought back to camp where the women broiled, roasted, or simply stewed it for fast eating. Otherwise, the deer meat was heavily salted and sun-dried for storage. Birds were also killed to be eaten, as well as for their feathers.

HUNTING AND FISHING

Hunting and fishing tools were the most important possessions tribal men owned. There were two kinds of hunting bows made by this tribe. One bow was made of wood wrapped in vegetable-fiber cord to keep it from breaking.

Wood for bows and arrows was carefully chosen and carved so arrows could accurately hit animals needed for food, and bows would not easily break.

The best bow Tubatulabal hunters made was of sinew-backed wood. Sinew is a stretchy tendon from animals of any size. When glued to a bow, sinew made it more bendable. Bendable wood made arrows go farther and did not break as easily after long use.

A

War arrows were from 34 inches to 36 inches long. These had a main shaft, usually of cane, with a pocket at one end. A smaller solid-wood shaft, with a stone point tied onto the front end, fitted into the pocket of the larger cane shaft. When this kind of arrow hit a target, only the front shaft and arrow point

Double-shafted arrows separate at A.

© Liddell 92

remained in the target (enemy), while the main shaft could be reused many times.

Hunting arrows were one-piece wood weapons which had been sharpened to a point on one end and hardened by fire. This type of arrow was four feet long. These arrows had to be constantly re-straightened so they would fly in a direct path toward their targets. Arrows were carried in quivers made of antelope, coyote, or wildcat hide.

Arrows were heated, then moved back and forth in a stone straightener until perfectly straight.

©72 Liddell

Single hunters stalked deer, wearing deerheads on their own heads to get closer to the animals. Hunters might group together to hunt. Tubatulabal hunters often joined with hunters of the Yokut tribe to kill antelope in the San Joaquin Valley.

There were also rabbit hunts where many hunters worked together. One group method for catching rabbits was to stretch a net across one end of a canyon, then set fire to brush at the other end. Rabbits were caught in the net as they tried to escape. Sometimes hunters would yell to scare rabbits into nets.

Tribal hunters learned to make sounds like a rabbit in trouble. When other rabbits heard the sound they would be shot as they came to help a rabbit signalling danger.

Traps, nets, snares, and throwing sticks were all used to catch smaller animals. Fishermen made nets, basket traps, bone and wood harpoons, fishhooks of bone, and wooden pens to catch fish.

A Tubatulabal hunter demonstrates how to call a rabbit sound.

© 92 Liddell

Most fishing was done alone. Only once a year, in July, did Tubatulabal fishermen work as a group. At that time, several villages joined together, making large stone dam traps, each shaped like a keyhole, in the rivers. The narrow end of a keyhole was left open. Sides of a keyhole were built up with stones and brush until they were above water level.

Men positioned themselves downstream from the trap, driving fish into it. Two men stationed at the narrow end of the keyhole grabbed the trapped fish and threw them onto the shore, where women clubbed them.

CLOTHING

Clothing was of little importance to tribal men and children because the weather was warm most of the year. Many of them wore no clothes, although women wore tanned deerhide skirts of double aprons, one in front and one in back.

In cooler weather buckskin vests were worn by both men and women, and men wore animal-hide loincloths. Both men and women also wore sleeveless coats of animal skin. During dry weather, while hunting and gathering food, tribal members wore buckskin moccasins with pitch on the soles.

Clowns, shamans, and all women wore ornaments or painted their bodies, only men (except shamans) did not. Women painted their faces red or white for dances and wore noseplugs, necklaces, and earrings. Women also tattooed themselves using a cactus spine to make a design by breaking the skin. Charcoal was the only dye used to color tattoos.

Shamans and clowns painted their faces in red and white stripes when they took part in contests or performed.

Ornaments used as nose plugs by the Tubatulabal women.

TOOLS

Tribal member used objects they found in nature as tools. Digging sticks were sturdy, three-feet-tall branches used to dig tubers and bulbs out of the ground. They were made of hardwood and had a sharp point on either end. Wood also provided materials for storage boxes, houses, and was used as fuel for fires.

Obsidian hide scraper.

Stone was used for hammers, mortars and pestles, and to line the sides of cooking ovens. Sharp-edged stone made good animal-hide scrapers. Obsidian (a volcanic glass) was chipped into sharp-edged arrow and spear points.

Tools were made from animal parts, also. Bone was used for whistles, and as ornaments for costumes; bone splinters

Bone whistle.

made excellent needles for sewing. Handles of black tar lumps were attached to large splinters of deer-leg bone, which became fine awls (sharply-pointed tools). These awls were strong, and sharp enough for flaking and shaping stone arrow points and knife blades.

Elastic animal tendons were not only used for strengthening wood, but also for thread when making clothes. Cactus spines made good needles for sewing clothing.

Root pieces of the soaproot plant could be used as soap to shampoo hair, or split into fibers as brushes to keep hair from tangling.

BASKETS AND POTTERY

Baskets filled most Tubatulabal women's needs to run their households. They were used in every part of tribal life. Women of this tribe made baskets using two types of weaving: twined and coiled.

41

Twined baskets, more loosely woven, were used as sieves, seed beaters, trays, storage baskets. The large burden baskets, carried on women's backs to haul heavy loads of food to their villages, were made by the open-twining method. There was also a Y-shaped twined cradle.

Twined basket.

Coiled baskets could be more tightly woven and were made for looks, as well as for need. Only coiled baskets had designs woven into them. Patterns on Tubatulabal baskets were usually geometric designs, sometimes of graphic snakes or humans.

Colors of designs depended on what plants were available. Tree-yucca roots were used for red patterns, pods of the devil's claw plant made a black-colored design. Brown and white colors were also used in basket patterns.

Basketry fish traps were made of woven tule sprouts. Other materials used by tribal women included split-willow or tree-yucca roots woven with deer grass.

Tubatulabal was one of only three California tribes that gathered clay to make pottery. The knowledge of how to make pottery probably came from Native American tribal women

Beautiful coiled basket with a geometric design.

in what is today Arizona State. Traders moving between the different tribes spread ideas, such as making pottery, from tribe to tribe.

California tribal women made their pottery bowls and jars by rolling clay into long round coils. The coils were laid on top of each other, then pinched together, sun-dried, and finally baked (or fired) in an open fire until the color was gray-black. Red clay from the South Fork Kern valley was the kind used by these tribal women when making pottery.

HISTORY

The first white people known to have visited the Tubatulabal tribe were explorers who came to the lower end of Kern Valley in 1776. For at least 50 years after that time, Tubatulabal traders made many long trips to Mission Buenaventura, on the Pacific Coast, to trade for products they wanted and needed.

By 1850, American settlers had taken over the Tubatulabal territory of all three of the Kern valleys. Ten years after the San Francisco gold rush, in 1857, miners discovered gold around the Kern River. The greedy miners succeeded in pushing what was left of the tribe completely off their own land.

In 1862, Tubatulabal men joined with another tribe to fight against white settlers in Owens Valley. American soldiers were called to help the settlers and several tribal men were killed.

By 1875, most Tubatulabal men were working on white settlers' ranches as laborers. In 1893 those tribal members still living in the area were given back some land in Kern and South Fork valleys. From 1900 to 1972 many Tubatulabal people moved onto the Tule River reservation. Others moved to cities, looking for jobs.

Today many still live in the Kern Valley area. Men work as cowhands, and women work as secretaries and accountants. Population of the tribe was thought to be around 1,000 before white people arrived. The 1972 census showed only 29 full-blooded Tubatulabal people still alive. At that time only six people still spoke the tribal language, and they were all over 50 years old.

Some native foods are still cooked for feasts. The custom of burning dead tribal members' clothes at funerals is still followed. In 1972, there was one 74-year-old shaman who was still being asked to cure everything but serious illness. We can only hope that young tribal members will keep their Tubatulabal heritage alive in the years to come.

TUBATULABAL TRIBE
OUTLINE

I. Introduction
    A. Meaning of the name
    B. Territory boundaries
        1. Description of territory and boundary markings
        2. Climate of territory
        3. Types of plant growth
        4. Language spoken

II. Villages
    A. Winter villages
        1. Dwelling house description
        2. Sweathouse description and use
    B. Summer campsites
        1. Brush shelters and framework description
    C. Nut-gathering campsites
        1. Description of brush enclosure

III. Village life
    A. Families
    B. Jobs of adults
        1. Tribal myth
    C. Marriage customs
        1. Three kinds of marriages
    D. Childbirth rituals
        1. Parents' food taboos
    E. Children's training
    F. Death customs
        1. Death rituals
        2. Mourning ceremony
        3. Beliefs of the dead ghosts
    G. Chiefs
        1. Duties
        2. How chosen
    H. Clown/dance-manager

IV. Wars and feuds
    A. War chief's duties
    B. Types of attacks
    C. Prisoners
V. Religion
    A. Supernatural spirits
    B. Shamans
        1. Both men and women
        2. Curing doctors and rituals
    C. Coyote power
    D. Dreams
VI. Food
    A. Plant food
        1. Piñon
            a. How theywere gathered
            b. How they were shelled
        2. Acorns
            a. How they were gathered and stored
        3. Berries and other plants
        4. Ways of cooking plants
    B. Meats
        1. Kinds eaten
        2. How prepared
VII. Hunting and fishing
    A. Hunting
        1. Bow and arrow descriptions
        2. Single and group hunts
        3. Nets and snares
        4. Small animals and rabbit hunts
    B. Fishing
        1. Single fishermen and tools
        2. Group fishing and keyhole trap
VIII. Clothing
    A. Men and children
    B. Women
    C. Cooler weather clothing
    D. Body paints and ornaments
    E. Tattoos

IX. Tools
  A. Wood tools
  B. Stone tools
  C. Animal parts for tools
X. Baskets and pottery
  A. Twined basket descriptions
    1. Uses
  B. Coiled basket descriptions
  C. Materials used for baskets and designs
  D. Pottery
    1. Kind of clay used
    2. Coil method of making pots
    3. Colors of pots
XI. History
  A. First white people to visit Tubatulabals
  B. Gold miners
  C. Fighting white settlers
  D. 1875, tribal ranch laborers
  E. Some land returned to tribe in 1893
  F. Tule River reservation
  G. The tribe today
    1. Uses

GLOSSARY

AWL: a sharp, pointed tool used for making small holes in leather or wood

CEREMONY: a meeting of people to perform formal rituals for a special reason; like an awards ceremony to hand out trophies to those who earned honors

CHERT: rock which can be chipped off, or flaked, into pieces with sharp edges

COILED: a way of weaving baskets which looks like the basket is made of rope coils woven together

DIAMETER: the length of a straight line through the center of a circle

DOWN: soft, fluffy feathers

DROUGHT: a long period of time without water

DWELLING: a building where people live

FLETCHING: attaching feathers to the back end of an arrow to make the arrow travel in a straight line

GILL NET: a flat net hanging vertically in water to catch fish by their heads and gills

GRANARIES: basket-type storehouses for grains and nuts

HERITAGE: something passed down to people from their long-ago relatives

LEACHING: washing away a bitter taste by pouring water through foods like acorn meal

MORTAR: flat surface of wood or stone used for the grinding of grains or herbs with a pestle

PARCHING: to toast or shrivel with dry heat

PESTLE: a small stone club used to mash, pound, or grind in a mortar

PINOLE: flour made from ground corn

INDIAN RESERVATION: land set aside for Native Americans by the United States government

RITUAL: a ceremony that is always performed the same way

SEINE NET: a net which hangs vertically in the water, encircling and trapping fish when it is pulled together

SHAMAN: tribal religious men or women who use magic to cure illness and speak to spirit-gods

SINEW: stretchy animal tendons

STEATITE: a soft stone (soapstone) mined on Catalina Island by the Gabrielino tribe; used for cooking pots and bowls

TABOO: something a person is forbidden to do

TERRITORY: land owned by someone or by a group of people

TRADITION: the handing down of customs, rituals, and belief, by word of mouth or example, from generation to generation

TREE PITCH: a sticky substance found on evergreen tree bark

TWINING: a method of weaving baskets by twisting fibers, rather than coiling them around a support fiber

NATIVE AMERICAN WORDS
WE KNOW AND USE

PLANTS AND TREES
hickory
pecan
yucca
mesquite
saguaro

ANIMALS
caribou
chipmunk
cougar
jaguar
opossum
moose

STATES
Dakota – friend
Ohio – good river
Minnesota – waters that
  reflect the sky
Oregon – beautiful water
Nebraska – flat water
Arizona
Texas

FOODS
avocado
hominy
maize (corn)
persimmon
tapioca
succotash

GEOGRAPHY
bayou – marshy body of
  water
savannah – grassy plain
pasadena – valley

WEATHER
blizzard
Chinook (warm, dry wind)

FURNITURE
hammock

HOUSE
wigwam
wickiup
tepee
igloo

INVENTIONS
toboggan

BOATS
canoe
kayak

OTHER WORDS
caucus – group meeting
mugwump – loner politician
squaw – woman
papoose – baby

CLOTHING
moccasin
parka
mukluk – slipper
poncho

BIBLIOGRAPHY

Cressman, L. S. *Prehistory of the Far West.* Salt Lake City, Utah: University of Utah Press, 1977.

Geiger, Maynard, O.F.M., Ph.D. *The Indians of Mission Santa Barbara.* Santa Barbara, CA 93105: Franciscan Fathers, 1986.

Heizer, Robert F., volume editor. *Handbook of North American Indians; California, volume 8.* Washington, D.C.: Smithsonian Institute, 1978.

Heizer, Robert F. and Elsasser, Albert B. *The Natural World of the California Indians.* Berkeley and Los Angeles, CA; London, England: University of California Press, 1980.

Heizer, Robert F. and Whipple, M.A.. *The California Indians.* Berkeley and Los Angeles, CA; London, England: University of California Press, 1971.

Heuser, Iva. *California Indians.* PO Box 352, Camino, CA 95709: Sierra Media Systems, 1977.

Macfarlen, Allen and Paulette. *Handbook of American Indian Games.* 31 E. 2nd Street, Mineola, N.Y. 11501: Dover Publications, 1985.

Murphey, Edith Van Allen. *Indian Uses of Native Plants.* 603 W. Perkins Street, Ukiah, CA 95482: Mendocino County Historical Society, © renewal, 1987.

National Geographic Society. *The World of American Indians.* Washington, DC: National Geographic Society reprint, 1989.

Tunis, Edwin. *Indians.* 2231 West 110th Street, Cleveland, OH: The World Publishing Company, 1959.

Credits:
Island Industries, Vashon Island, Washington 98070
Dona McAdam, Mac on the Hill, Seattle, Washington 98109

Acknowledgements:
Kim Walters, Library Director, and Richard Buchen,
Research Librarian, Braun Library, Southwest Museum
Special thanks

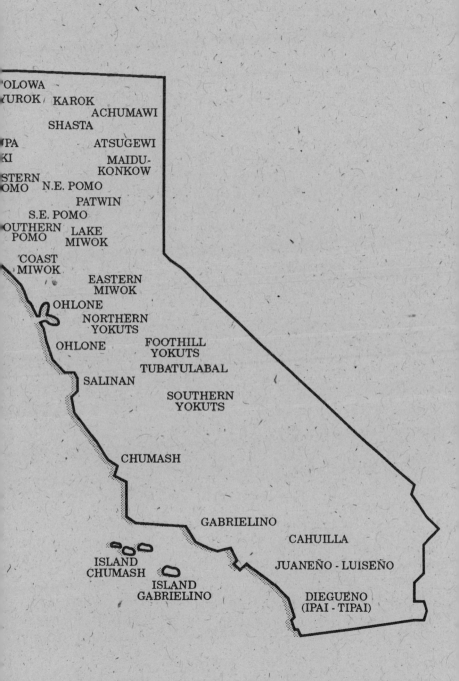

OLOWA
YUROK KAROK
        ACHUMAWI
  SHASTA
PA   ATSUGEWI
KI
        MAIDU-
        KONKOW
STERN
OMO   N.E. POMO
      PATWIN
  S.E. POMO
OUTHERN   LAKE
 POMO   MIWOK
  COAST
  MIWOK
      EASTERN
      MIWOK
   OHLONE
    NORTHERN
    YOKUTS
  OHLONE   FOOTHILL
          YOKUTS
       TUBATULABAL
  SALINAN
       SOUTHERN
       YOKUTS

  CHUMASH

        GABRIELINO
           CAHUILLA
  ISLAND   JUANEÑO - LUISEÑO
  CHUMASH
    ISLAND
    GABRIELINO   DIEGUENO
            (IPAI - TIPAI)

Map Art: Dona McAdam

At last, a detailed book on the
Tubatulabal Tribe
written just for students

Mary Null Boulé taught in the California
public school system for twenty-five years.
Her teaching years made her aware of the
acute need for well-researched regional
social studies books for elementary school
students. This series on the California
Native American tribes fills a long-standing
need in California education. Ms. Boulé is
also author and publisher of *The Missions:
California's Heritage.* She is married and
the mother of five grown children.

Illustrator Daniel Liddell has been creating
artistic replicas of Native American arti-
facts for several years, and his paintings
reflect his own Native American heritage.
His paternal grandmother was full-blood
Chickasaw.

ISBN: 1-877599-24-7